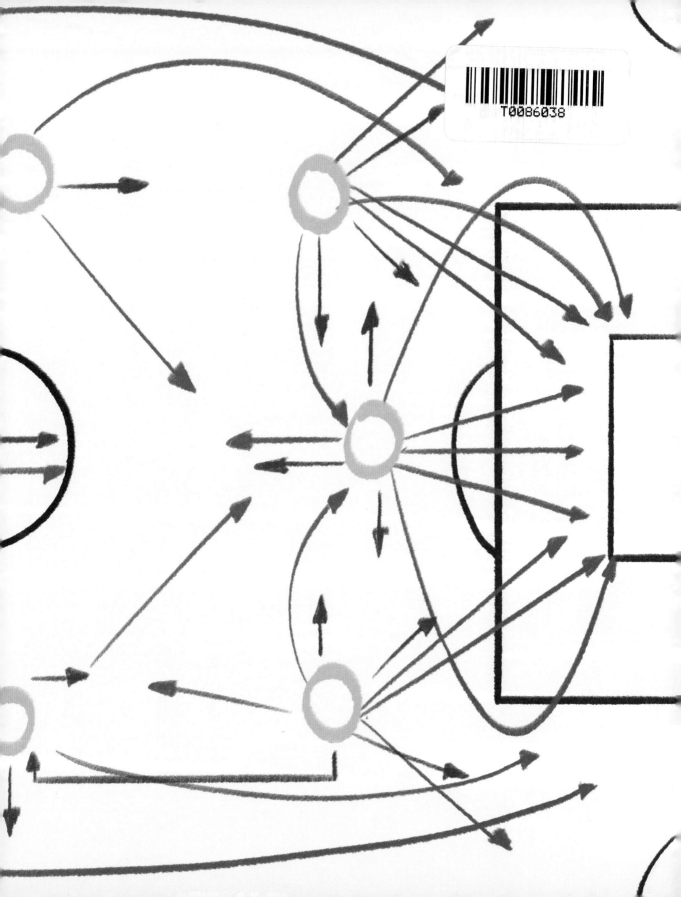

Little People, BIG DREAMS®
JÜRGEN KLOPP

Written by
Maria Isabel Sánchez Vegara

Illustrated by
Beatriz Castro

Frances Lincoln
Children's Books

Once, in a little German village deep inside the Black Forest, lived a boy called Jürgen. He loved skiing during the winter, playing tennis in the summer and practising football all year round. It was his favourite sport!

Jürgen joined the local football club, and soon his enthusiasm earned him the title of captain.

He was a natural leader, always ready to inspire others.
But even the best players miss the goal sometimes...

As a Stuttgart fan, he never missed a match on the radio. Just by listening to the game, Jürgen knew which players should be switched for the team to win. And most of the time, those were the changes the coach would make next!

He was studying sports science at university when he got the chance to play as a forward for a small team called Mainz 05. Jürgen wasn't the best player, but his passion and commitment, even when losing, made him the fans' favourite.

Soon, Jürgen realised that the best way to help his team win a match was not on the field but from the bench. So, twice a week, he travelled 120 miles to the German Sport University to learn everything he needed to become a coach.

His chance came sooner than expected when Mainz 05's manager was sacked just two days before an important game. The club was about to be moved down from the second to the third division when Jürgen agreed to coach the team.

Thanks to Jürgen, the club stayed in the second tier.
Then, two seasons later, they made it into the Bundesliga,
the German first division. His team had the smallest budget
and the tiniest stadium, but they played like true champions.

His next challenge as a manager was helping Borussia Dortmund – one of the biggest teams in Germany – to win titles again. Jürgen taught his players that by working as a team and helping one another, anything was possible!

Of course, they did not always win, and that was all right. Instead of feeling disappointed, Jürgen stayed positive. He took every defeat as a chance to improve. That's how his squad became the youngest ever to win the Bundesliga.

Every club in Europe wanted Jürgen to lead their team,
but there was one who needed him desperately: Liverpool.
As soon as he became their boss he sent a message to
the supporters: to change from doubters to believers.

His unique personality inspired players, made journalists laugh and brought confidence back to Liverpool's fans. Jürgen led the team to their first Premier League victory in 30 years and a long-awaited European Cup.

That year he was named the best men's coach by FIFA, football's world organisation. But success never changed his humble nature. He always knew what really mattered – like the team's yearly visit to the local children's hospital.

And little Jürgen, the kid who dreamt of being a footballer, realised there is something even better than scoring the final goal.

It is being the person who inspires everyone to do better as a team.

JÜRGEN KLOPP

(Born 1967)

1999   2004

Jürgen Norbert Klopp grew up in Glatten, a small village in Germany's
Black Forest. Encouraged by his parents, Jürgen spent his childhood
playing, watching and listening to a variety of sports, but his passion was
football. He thought strategically about the game from a young age and
captained Glatten's youth teams. Jürgen was a natural leader – ambitious,
determined and always honest with his teammates. In his late teens, he
played for TuS Ergenzingen as a junior and then went to university to study
sports science. Here, Jürgen's tactical approach and athleticism lead him
to play successfully for several amateur clubs and sign with the German
second division team, Mainz 05, where he played 325 games over the next
eleven years. His chance to lead the team came when they were left without

2008   2022

a manager shortly before an important game against MSV Duisburg.
They risked being relegated to the third division, but Jürgen stepped in to
coach and they won! With Jürgen in charge, Mainz 05 were promoted
to the Bundesliga for the first time in their history. Next, he moved to
manage the German first division team, Borussia Dortmund, who won the
Bundesliga title just three years later. In 2015 Jürgen joined Liverpool FC.
The English club became European champions under his leadership and
continue to add to their trophies. Jürgen is an inspiration and mentor to
both players and fans. He has recieved The Best FIFA Men's Coach Award
twice and was the first Premier League manager to pledge 1% of his salary
to charity. Jürgen's story reminds us that shared success is the sweetest of all.

Want to find out more about **Jürgen Klopp?**

Have a read of this great book:

Football School Epic Heroes
by Alex Bellos, Ben Lyttleton and Spike Gerrell

Published by Peter Marley · Designed by Sasha Moxon
Commissioned by Lucy Menzies · Edited by Molly Mead
Production by Nikki Ingram

Manufactured in Guangdong, China CC082023
1 3 5 7 9 8 6 4 2

Photographic acknowledgements (pages 28-29, from left to right): 1) Hamburg, Germany – October 24: 2. Bundesliga 99/00,
Hamburg; FC St. Pauli – FSV Mainz 05 2:2; Jürgen Kramny/Mainz, Zlatan Bajramovic/St.Pauli, Jürgen Klopp/Mainz © Elisenda Roig/
Bongarts via Getty Images. 2) Fussball: 2. Bundesliga 03/04, Mainz; Aufstieg 1. FSV Mainz 05 in die 1. Bundesliga; Trainer Jürgen
Klopp/Mainz feiert auf dem Marktplatz 23.05.04 © Moritz Winde/Bongarts via Getty Images. 3) Klopp, Jürgen – Coach, Borussia
Dortmund, Germany – talking to his players during first training session of season 2008–2009 © Team 2 Sportphoto/ullstein bild via
Getty Images. 4) Jürgen Klopp the head coach/manager of Liverpool celebrates winning the Emirates FA Cup during the final match
between Chelsea and Liverpool at Wembley Stadium on May 14, 2022 in London, England
© Matthew Ashton – AMA via Getty Images.

Collect the *Little People,* **BIG DREAMS**® series:

FRIDA KAHLO · COCO CHANEL · MAYA ANGELOU · AMELIA EARHART · AGATHA CHRISTIE · MARIE CURIE · ROSA PARKS · AUDREY HEPBURN

EMMELINE PANKHURST · ELLA FITZGERALD · ADA LOVELACE · JANE AUSTEN · GEORGIA O'KEEFFE · HARRIET TUBMAN · ANNE FRANK · MOTHER TERESA

JOSEPHINE BAKER · L. M. MONTGOMERY · JANE GOODALL · SIMONE DE BEAUVOIR · MUHAMMAD ALI · STEPHEN HAWKING · MARIA MONTESSORI · VIVIENNE WESTWOOD

MAHATMA GANDHI · DAVID BOWIE · WILMA RUDOLPH · DOLLY PARTON · BRUCE LEE · RUDOLF NUREYEV · ZAHA HADID · MARY SHELLEY

MARTIN LUTHER KING JR. · DAVID ATTENBOROUGH · ASTRID LINDGREN · EVONNE GOOLAGONG · BOB DYLAN · ALAN TURING · BILLIE JEAN KING · GRETA THUNBERG

JESSE OWENS · JEAN-MICHEL BASQUIAT · ARETHA FRANKLIN · CORAZON AQUINO · PELÉ · ERNEST SHACKLETON · STEVE JOBS · AYRTON SENNA

LOUISE BOURGEOIS · ELTON JOHN · JOHN LENNON · PRINCE · CHARLES DARWIN · CAPTAIN TOM MOORE · HANS CHRISTIAN ANDERSEN · STEVIE WONDER

MEGAN RAPINOE · MARY ANNING · MALALA YOUSAFZAI · ANDY WARHOL · RUPAUL · MICHELLE OBAMA · MINDY KALING · IRIS APFEL

ROSALIND FRANKLIN · RUTH BADER GINSBURG · MARILYN MONROE · KAMALA HARRIS · ALBERT EINSTEIN · CHARLES DICKENS · YOKO ONO · MICHAEL JORDAN

NELSON MANDELA · PABLO PICASSO · AMANDA GORMAN · GLORIA STEINEM · FLORENCE NIGHTINGALE · HARRY HOUDINI · J.R.R. TOLKIEN · ELVIS PRESLEY

NEIL ARMSTRONG · ALEXANDER VON HUMBOLDT · NIKOLA TESLA · WILMA MANKILLER · MARCUS RASHFORD · LAVERNE COX · MAE JEMISON · DWAYNE JOHNSON

HELEN KELLER · ANNA PAVLOVA · QUEEN ELIZABETH · TERRY FOX · HEDY LAMARR · SHAKIRA · FREDDIE MERCURY · LEWIS HAMILTON

LOUIS PASTEUR · PRINCESS DIANA · DAVID HOCKNEY · VANESSA NAKATE · OLIVE MORRIS · KING CHARLES

MOZART · STEVE IRWIN · JÜRGEN KLOPP · LEO MESSI

Scan the QR code for free activity sheets, teachers' notes and more information about the series at www.littlepeoplebigdreams.com

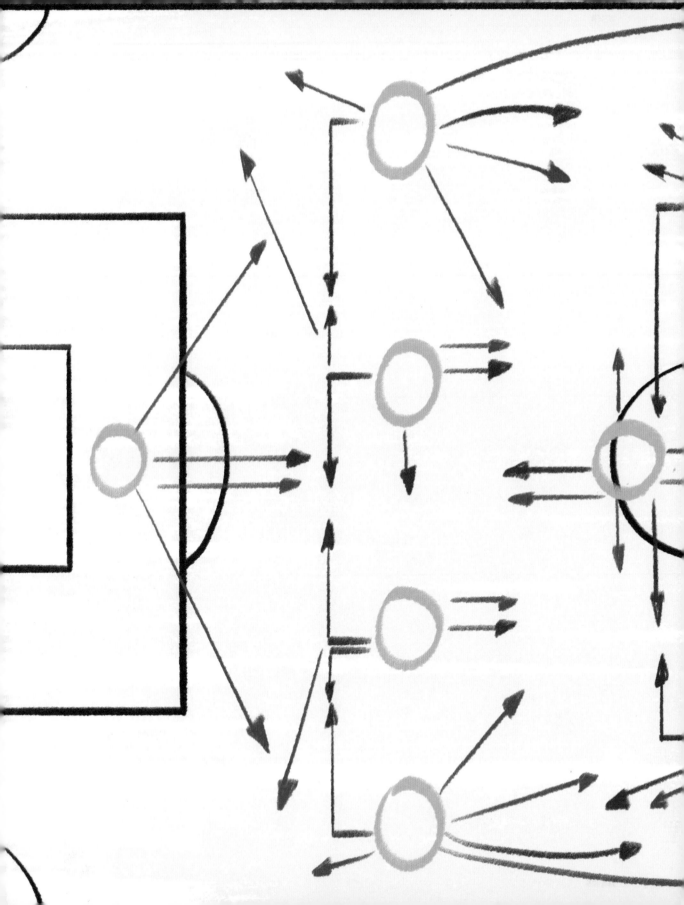